BRITAIN'S DMUs: 1986–2022

GEORGE WOODS

AMBERLEY

First published 2024

Amberley Publishing
The Hill, Stroud
Gloucestershire, GL5 4EP

www.amberley-books.com

Copyright © George Woods, 2024

The right of George Woods to be identified as
the Author of this work has been asserted in
accordance with the Copyrights, Designs and
Patents Act 1988.

ISBN 978 1 3981 1568 2 (print)
ISBN 978 1 3981 1569 9 (ebook)

British Library Cataloguing in Publication Data.
A catalogue record for this book is available from
the British Library.

Origination by Amberley Publishing.
Printed in the UK.

Introduction

By the early 1980s the original fleet of DMUs that had entered service in the late 1950s and the 1960s were beginning to show their age, and becoming due for replacement. Some types, such as the Met-Cam 101 and the Derby-built Class 108, were refurbished to extend their use for another few years, but the majority went to the scrapyard, while some entered Departmental use and several were purchased by heritage railways.

The search for replacements started with the Class 140 railbus, which was developed with British Leyland. The bodywork was a development of the Leyland National bus, running on an improved four-wheel wagon chassis, and powered by a 200-hp Leyland engine. A prototype was constructed at Derby in 1980, which would prove to be the forerunner of the Pacer family of trains. It saw very little public service and eventually, after much trial running and being used as the Neville Hill depot driver training vehicle, it was preserved on the Keith & Dufftown Railway in the north of Scotland in 1990.

The prototype was seen as relatively successful, which led to the first production model Pacer trains, powered by two Leyland 205-hp engines, resulting in twenty of the Class 141 being built at Derby in 1984, entering service on routes served by Neville Hill depot in Leeds, remaining in service until 1997. On withdrawal, twelve of the 141s were sold to Iran Railways where they lasted in service for eight years.

BR was under pressure to come up with a cheap and cheerful design for use on little-used rural branch lines and short-distance urban routes, so the Pacer Class 141 was developed into classes 142, 143 and 144 of two- and three-car units. Class 142 was introduced in 1985, and ninety-six two-car units were put into service mainly on Lancashire and Yorkshire routes. They were very similar to the 141s except that the body was wider, but the rough ride over jointed track remained, which meant that they were never popular with passengers, resulting in them gaining the nickname of 'Nodding Donkeys'. The next development was Class 143, which was much the same but with an improved exterior and an uprated suspension, which did not make much difference owing to the basic freight wagon underpinnings of the original design.

In 1986 the final development of the Pacer, the Class 144, was put into service, which included ten three-car units. Along with the rest of the Pacers, the Achilles' heel was the transmission, which was very unreliable and was not fixed until a replacement was found. At the same time more powerful engines were fitted, all of which took several years to implement but resulted in improved reliability.

Withdrawal of all the Pacers was met with great relief by the travelling public as in their final years they became very tatty and leaked water in heavy rain. Some train companies wanted to keep using them but the introduction of regulations regarding the carriage of disabled persons, which required a level entry to allow wheelchair access to all trains, was the final straw as they had quite a steep entry step, and in 2020 the last one was taken out of service. Not surprisingly some fifty units have survived in use on heritage railways, as they are ideal for use on off-peak services, but it will be interesting to see the public reaction to them.

In 1984 the prototype Class 150 DMU known as Sprinter units, developed by BR at York, were introduced. Two prototypes were built, one with Cummins and the second with Perkins engines, and two different transmissions. They both had underfloor engines and consisted of three cars but were internally of poor design with badly spaced passenger accommodation with little provision for luggage. They went into competition with another prototype built by Met-Cam, the Class 151, also a three-car unit, but their production was delayed. Eventually after trials of both types, the Class 150 proved to be superior, having excellent riding, and the Cummins engine proved the more reliable, resulting in an order for 135 two- and three-car units, which were produced in two batches between 1984 and 1987. These units have given sterling service despite their shortcomings and are still in service on many parts of the network, but are due for replacement in the near future.

The next type to be introduced was the Class 155, which was intended for medium-distance journeys, and forty-two two-car sets were built by British Leyland in 1987–88 which used similar lighter body construction to those used in the railbuses. After entering service, problems arose with the sliding doors, but when these were fixed they proved reliable performers.

Because of problems with the railbuses on routes with sharp curves, and the need to replace ageing Class 121 and 122 units, it was decided to rebuild the 155s into single-car units, which became Class 153. These units had bogies and were much better suited to working the more curvaceous routes and other lightly used services. Seven Class 155 units used by West Yorkshire PTE were not converted as they wished to retain them for their services. Most Class 153s are still in service, and the remaining 155s are now based at Hull for local services in that area.

One of the most important requirements was for the longer-distance Regional Railways services such as Leeds to Carlisle, Norwich to Birmingham and Glasgow to Mallaig, which were not suitable to be served by InterCity-type trains. The outcome was the introduction of the Class 156 Super Sprinter. One hundred and fourteen two-car sets with a top speed of 75 mph were built in 1987–89 by Metro-Cammell, and the first entered service in 1988. These were a great improvement on the Class 150 and remain in service today and with many TOCs throughout the network.

For limited stop long-distance Regional Railways routes, the Class 158/159 Express Sprinter was introduced in 1990. Constructed by British Rail Engineering at Derby, it was built with a welded aluminium body and was designed to run at a top speed of 90 mph and to offer superior comfort to earlier types of DMU. A total of 182 two- and three-car units were built, and were powered by Cummins or Perkins diesel engines, and fitted with air conditioning. They can be found on services as far north as Inverness to Wick and Thurso, many routes in Wales, the Midlands, East Anglia and as far west as Plymouth.

In 1992, twenty-two Class 158s were converted to three-car Class 159 units by Babcock Rail in Rosyth, to replace elderly loco-hauled trains on the Waterloo to Salisbury and Exeter routes, and in 2007 another seven units were added to work expanded services in Hampshire.

The Class 158 and 159 can be counted as one of British Rails' success stories as they continue to give reliable service to many TOCs all over the network.

In 1991/2 seventy-six Class 165 and 165/1 Network Turbo two- and three-car units were built for the Network Southeast Chiltern Line and Thames Valley line services at York Works. Then in 1992/3 Class 166, which was a faster three-car train for longer-distance services in the Thames Valley and also fitted with air conditioning, were also built at York. Both 165 and 166 are powered by Perkins diesel engines.

The next development was the Class 170 Turbostar, which was intended to take over some of the longer-distance services from the 158s, and a total of 139 two- and three-car units were built by Adtranz and Bombardier at Derby between 1998 and 2005. Scotrail have been the biggest user of these units and employed them on Edinburgh/Glasgow to Inverness and Aberdeen routes, as well as some shorter-distance heavily used services such as Edinburgh to Glasgow.

After the electrification of some Scottish services, Class 170s have found their way south, and are now employed on services such as Sheffield to Scarborough via Hull. East Midlands and West Midlands have also gained some of these units, as have CrossCountry trains and TransPennine. Earlier users include Hull Trains and Anglia, while Chiltern Trains use similar Class 168 on their services from Marylebone to Birmingham, with Southern using Class 171 on South Coast services. Another member of the Turbostar family is the Class 172, and thirty-nine two- and three-car sets were built in 2010/11 for the West Midlands Railway for use in the Birmingham area.

Despite opposition from the Department for Transport, Northern Rail were keen to phase out the Pacer units and selected the Class 195, which is manufactured in Spain and Newport, South Wales by CAF, resulting in an order for fifty-eight two- and three-car units in 2016 with construction beginning in 2017. The order was completed in 2021 with the trains now in service throughout the North West.

This more or less brings the BR DMU story up to date. It all started nearly seventy years ago in 1955 with the Derby Lightweight units and finishes with the Class 195. New Class 196/197 trains are coming on stream with West Midlands and Transport for Wales, and Anglia have taken delivery of Class 755 Bi-mode units, but I have not yet managed to get to see them. Maybe something for volume three.

Abbreviations

CAF	Construcciones y Auxiliar de Ferrocarriles
DMU	Diesel Multiple Unit
GMPTE	Greater Manchester Passenger Transport Executive
GNER	Great North Eastern Railway
LNWR	London North Western Railways
L&YR	Lancashire and Yorkshire Railway
Met-Cam	Metropolitan Cammell
NYMR	North Yorkshire Moors Railway
SPT	Strathclyde Partnership for Transport
TOC	Train Operating Company
TMD	Traction Maintenance Depot
TPE	TransPennine Express
WYPTE	West Yorkshire Passenger Transport Executive

This prototype Pacer unit has been in preservation at the Keith & Dufftown Railway in the north of Scotland since February 1995. Seen here at Dufftown on 24 June 2003.

An almost brand-new 141 001 is stabled at the York TMD in August 1984.

Two Regional Railways Class 142 units and a WYPTE Class 144 run alongside the River Derwent near Kirkham Abbey, with a Leeds to Scarborough train, on 25 April 1987.

142 015 is seen at York station in October 1989. This unit was originally part of Regional Railways Devon and Cornwall fleet, where they were known as 'Skippers', but they had to be relocated to services in the north of England, as the long wheelbase was unsuited to West Country branch lines with their sharp curves.

142 086 passes the Midland Railway signal box at Settle Junction with a Leeds to Morecambe service on a frosty 25 November 1989.

A pair of 156 units led by 156 451 depart from Chesterfield with a Regional Railways service to Liverpool on 29 September 1990. The famous crooked church spire of St Mary and All Saints stands out on the skyline.

On a very wintry morning in February 1991, 158 754 departs from York with a Manchester Airport to Newcastle service.

The original Track Recording Unit (TRU) D999600/01 is stabled at York station for the weekend in June 1991. The two-car set was adapted from the last Class 150/0 to be constructed.

A Chester to Wolverhampton service formed of Regional Railways 150 119 passes through Weston Rhyn on 12 October 1990.

On 23 September 1991, Central Trains three-car 150 108 is seen calling at Welshpool station with a Pwllheli to Wolverhampton train. The railway as seen here was moved to the other side of the original station building to allow construction of a bypass road, which opened in 1993.

Two refurbished Class 159 units, with 159 021 nearest the camera, stand in the sidings at York station in August 1991. They are on their way from the Rosyth Dockyard, where they were converted from Class 158, to their operators, Network South East, who will use them on Waterloo to Exeter services.

Class 156 404 arrives at Ely station, still with its semaphore signals, with a train for Manchester Piccadilly on 19 October 1991. Signs of the impending electrification from Cambridge to King's Lynn are evident, with electric services starting on 28 July 1992.

So good they numbered it twice. 150 150 arrives at Carnforth passing a nice set of semaphore signals with a service for Lancaster in June 1992.

More semaphore signals, this time at Barrow-in-Furness station where 153 360 arrives with a service from Carlisle on 15 April 1995.

Two units seen on a Sunday morning at York station in January 1998. On the left is Regional Railways 153 328 and alongside is Tyne and Wear 142 019, which is some way from home.

Another Tyne and Wear unit, this time 143 120, also seen at York in October 1991 on a special working.

GMPTE 142 013 calls at Ulleskelf with a Manchester Victoria to York service on 7 November 1992. At this time very few trains stopped here, but I managed a lucky photo while awaiting double-headed Class 50s on a special.

Metro Train 144 014, working a York to Sheffield service, bumps over the crossings at Monk Fryston on 17 March 1997. The first thirteen 144s were built as two-car sets, but this is one of ten which were built as three-car sets in 1987.

Another shot at Monk Fryston on 7 July 1996 sees a well-loaded 142 096 also on a York to Sheffield train.

150 219 speeds past the site of South Brent station on 12 July 1996 with an Exeter to Plymouth service. The station, which was the junction for the branch line to Kingsbridge, closed in 1964.

Above and below: Two pictures showing viaducts on the Settle and Carlisle line. The photo above shows a Class 156 heading a northbound service for Carlisle across the 130-foot-high Smardale Viaduct on 23 July 1994, and below a Class 142 and 156 cross the 117-foot-high Arten Gill Viaduct also heading for Carlisle on 29 March 1997.

Class 158 765 starts the climb out of Bradford Interchange station with a York to Manchester Victoria train in July 1997.

A York to Sheffield service formed of 144 005 passes through Monk Fryston on 17 March 1997. The station here closed in 1959.

150 271 has just departed from Stainforth and Hatfield station on 12 September 1999 with a Doncaster to Hull train. It is passing Hatfield Colliery, which was one of the last collieries in Yorkshire, closing in 2015.

At Colton Junction near York, the TransPennine Express thoroughbred 158 743 easily outpaces Arriva 'Nodding Donkey' 142 071, pictured in October 2001.

The North Eastern Railway atmosphere survives at Bridlington station with the signal box and goods shed seen in the left background of the picture, and many parts of the 1912 station still very much intact, as it is today. 142 083 waits to depart with a service for Hull.

At Scarborough the NER atmosphere also survives, as 158 803 arrives with a train from Manchester Airport passing Falsgrave signal box, and under the famous signal gantry which survives in use at Pickering on the NYMR.

On 12 September 1999 still on the North Eastern, this time at Hull station, which is seen from the Park Street bridge, a Class 158 departs for Sheffield passing the coaches of a special train. The original station dates from 1847, but in 1904 it was rebuilt by the NER. In 2007 the number of platforms were reduced to make way for a bus station alongside the station.

Also at Hull on the same day but looking in the other direction, 156 468 in its original Regional Railways Super Sprinter livery arrives with a train from Manchester.

Midland Mainline 170 101 waits at St Pancras to work a northbound service in June 2000.

Central Trains 170 514 passes a field of poppies at Melton Ross while working a Nottingham to Cleethorpes service.

Seen at Stratford station in September 2000, 170 202 is working the short-lived Anglia service from Basingstoke to Norwich, which operated from May 2000 until September 2002.

Another short-lived experiment was the Midland Mainline service from St Pancras to Sheffield, which on summer Saturdays was extended to York and Scarborough. 170 116 is seen here passing Colton on 6 April 2002 making for St Pancras.

Great Western 166 203–209 stand in Paddington station on 17 April 2002 with services to Oxford.

At Reading station 165 111 waits to depart for Basingstoke with a stopping train on 17 April 2002.

Threading its way through a sea of semaphores at Wrawton Junction, Barnetby, 158 763 makes for Cleethorpes with a train from Manchester on 22 May 2002. The area was resignalled in January 2016 using the latest digital colour light equipment.

Central Trains 150 109 runs through the hawthorn blossom at Melton Ross with a Cleethorpes to Nottingham service on 22 May 2002.

Central Trains 156 414 departs from Barnetby with a Nottingham to Grimsby service on 22 May 2002.

Northern Trains 158 806 passes Towthorpe, on the outskirts of York, with a Scarborough to Liverpool service in October 2002.

A North Western 175 007 Coradia unit passes Winwick with a northbound service on 31 May 2003.

168 106 departs from Princes Risborough with a Chiltern Railways Marylebone to Birmingham service on 5 June 2003.

Above and below: Two pictures taken at Appleby station of Northern Trains Carlisle to Leeds services taken on 12 June 2003. The picture above shows 158 909 heading south, and below later in the day 156 490 follows.

Above and below: Scotrail trains feature in both pictures on this page. Above at Mallaig station a pair of Class 156 units led by 156 474 wait at to make the 164-mile journey to Glasgow Queen Street on 18 June 2003, and below waiting to depart from Aviemore station is 158 740 with a service from Inverness to Glasgow Queen Street taken on 21 June 2003.

153 358 arrives at Ulverston station in June 2000 with a Lancaster to Barrow service. The station is unusual as the northbound track has platform access from both sides of the train.

156 473 climbs away from Birkett Tunnel with a train from Carlisle to Leeds on 11 October 2003.

Above and below: Two views of Northern trains on the Settle and Carlisle line taken on 14 February 2004. Above 158 905 passes Helwith Bridge with a Carlisle service, and below 156 488 calls at Settle station with a Carlisle-bound train.

TransPennine Express 158 763 passes through Towthorpe, on the outskirts of York, with a Scarborough to Liverpool service on 7 June 2004.

On 20 July 2004, a Northern Class 156 unit crosses the River Ouse at York with a train for Scarborough. The towpath at this point is a popular mooring point for the many boats that pass up and down the river.

Above and below: Two Class 170 units seen in London Terminals. 170 393 stands at platform eleven in the suburban part of Kings Cross on 2 June 2004 waiting to head north with a Hull Trains service. Four stops around the Circle Line at Liverpool Street station 170 207 waits to depart for Yarmouth with an Anglia Trains service. Both of these services have seen many changes of rolling stock over the past twenty years.

Great Western 165 130 shortly after leaving Twyford station on 3 June 2004 with a Reading to Paddington service.

At Reading station Great Western 165 137 and South West Trains 170 303 wait to form services to Newbury and Basingstoke on 3 June 2004.

This picture of 158 825 undergoing repairs was taken in Crewe Works during the open day held on 10 September 2005. The unit was run by Arriva Wessex Trains and has adverts for Ginsters.

Outside the works on the same day, 143 613 has suffered serious fire damage and was later scrapped at Cardiff Canton TMD.

Arriva Metro 144 019 stands in York station waiting to work a Harrogate service in March 2004.

A Manchester to Windermere train formed of 175 113 waits to depart from Oxenholme station on 22 April 2006.

Above and below: The next five pictures show the five liveries worn by Class 156 units working in Scotland since privatisation, all photographed at Carlisle station. The above picture shows 156 456 in the original Scotrail livery, and below 156 449 is in the second, waiting to depart for Glasgow Central via Dumfries, both photographed on 6 September 2006.

Above and below: Above, The third and current Saltire livery is worn by 156 439, seen departing for Glasgow via Dumfries on 2 August 2011. Below, 156 512, in the first SPT livery, waits to depart for Stranraer Harbour in October 1991.

The second SPT livery is seen on 156 442, which is waiting to depart for Dumfries. Standing alongside is 86901, which was part of the Network Rail fleet but was scrapped in June 2018 by Booths at Rotherham. Taken on 16 August 2006.

In mid-2006 there was a big switch round of units between various TOCs, and Northern received a variety of colourful Class 158 units including this Central Trains 158 794, seen here at Carlisle on 6 September 2006 waiting to depart for Leeds.

An Arriva Wales Class 158 crosses the Barmouth Viaduct with a Wolverhampton to Pwllheli service on 18 September 2006.

South West 158 786 leads several sister units out of Clapham Junction station on 10 September 2006 with a Salisbury to Waterloo service.

This is the only time I have seen a Class 150 working a Carlisle to Leeds train. The last train of the day on 29 April 2006 is formed of 150 140 and is approaching Birkett Tunnel.

The trains were usually formed of Class 156 units, and in this photo the mid-afternoon train to Leeds is formed of 156 454/469 about to cross Lunds Viaduct and enter Moorcock Tunnel on 6 May 2006.

On 23 September 2006 a small exhibition of modern railway rolling stock was held at Darlington station, which included 156 461, advertising the Ravenglass & Eskdale Railway.

Pacer 142 024 waits at Darlington station on 23 September 2006 to form a service to Saltburn-by-the-Sea.

Another service that used Pacer units was the Cumbrian Coast line from Carlisle to Barrow. Merseyrail 142 047 is a long way from its usual haunts at Carlisle, waiting to work down to Barrow on 6 September 2006.

Leeds is the eleventh busiest BR station, and by the 1990s congestion was causing delays, which got so bad that a major operation lasting three years from 1999 to 2002 was carried out to remodel the track layout and improve the station facilities. This picture was taken at dusk on 1 November 2006 at Leeds station with 150 279 waiting to form a westbound departure.

Above and below: Two pictures taken on 26 September 2006 of Class 156 units at Appleby station both working trains to Leeds. Above 156 481 is seen in the standard green on blue colours, and below 156 425 wears the short-lived mauve and white livery.

At Edinburgh Waverley station on 29 December 2006, 158 723 waits to depart with a northbound service. The train stands at platform one, which was created during improvements to the station in readiness for electrification of many local services.

SPT 156 502 departs from Glasgow Central on 23 February 2007 with a service for Barrhead.

153 352 plus a Class 156 unit have just come over the 1,169-foot summit at Ais Gill and catch the sun as they approach the short Shotlock Hill Tunnel with a Carlisle to Leeds train on 30 September 2006.

158 908/906 climb past Birkett Common with a Carlisle to Leeds service on 12 May 2007. Both units are in the latest WYPTE Metro livery.

At Appleby station 158 842 and a strengthening Class 153 on the front depart for Leeds on 12 May 2007. 158 842 had recently arrived at Northern trains from Arriva Wales in the reshuffle of units.

Formerly belonging to Wessex Trains and still wearing its Celebrating Brunel livery, 158 860 is far from its original home. Transferred to Northern, it is seen at Appleby working a Settle and Carlisle train to Carlisle on 6 September 2007.

On a glorious afternoon 158 792 has just left Langwathby heading south with a Carlisle to Leeds service. This unit is in the new Northern livery advertising places in the north to visit by train, which were appearing on units at this time.

Yet another new Northern livery is seen on 158 849 departing from Carlisle with the 15.05 to Leeds on 19 December 2007.

156 506 departs from Ayr with a train for Kilmarnock on 11 September 2007. Ayr station was built by the Glasgow & South Western Railway in 1886.

A Glasgow Central to Stranraer train formed of 156 478 arrives at Barrhill station on 13 September 2007. The train is about to pass the tiny signal cabin which controls the passing loop at this station.

Above and below: Two pictures taken at Glasgow Central on 25 February 2011. The above picture shows the view looking across the bridge over the River Clyde with trains arriving and departing. Below 158 701 arrives with a local service. Central station was opened by the Caledonian Railway in 1879 and was enlarged to its current size in 1905, and has seventeen platforms including two in the low-level station.

Above and below: Two pictures taken in the North East of Bishop Auckland to Saltburn trains on 17 September 2007. Above, 142 084 departs from Shildon station passing an interesting collection of old railway buildings. Below, 142 091 stands in the magnificent Darlington Bank Top station Opened in 1887 by the North Eastern Railway, this is the third station, as the previous two became inadequate for the contemporary traffic levels.

142 087 passes under the unusual NER signal box as it arrives at Hexham with a Tyne Valley line train from Newcastle on 8 September 2007.

At Leeds station on 9 May 2007, 158 902 departs with a York to Blackpool North train. In the background a GNER service waits to depart for Kings Cross.

Above and below: Two pictures taken at Ravenglass station on 22 September 2007 which is on the Cumbrian Coast line from Barrow to Carlisle. The above picture shows the former 1875 Furness station building, which is now a pub called the Ratty Arms, with a train for Barrow formed of 153 360 and 156 480 about to head north. The lower picture shows 156 420 departing south for Barrow. To the right of the picture, the Ravenglass and Eskdale narrow-gauge railway station and yard can be seen complete with two old Pullman cars, a preserved Cumberland bus, and a very nice red Datsun 240Z sports car.

On 1 March 2008 at Weston Super Mare station 143 619 waits to depart with a train for Bristol Parkway. The station and other facilities here have been greatly reduced in size since the 1960s when Weston was a major resort both for day-trippers and holidaymakers.

Fresh from the paint shop, GWR 153 372 waits to depart from Bristol Temple Meads on 1 March 2008 with the 11.13 to Severn Beach.

Above and below: Two pictures taken on 13 March 2008 of Leeds to Carlisle trains at Blea Moor. The picture above was taken looking south showing 158 843 with the top of the 2,372-foot Ingleborough lost in the cloud. Below, 158 790 is running through the cutting on the approach to Blea Moor Tunnel, which can be seen ahead.

Doing its best to disappear into the murk and rain, a 153/158 combination crosses the Ribblehead Viaduct on 13 March 2008 making for Leeds. The viaduct, at a height of 104 feet and 440 yards long, is the biggest on the Settle and Carlisle line.

Coming through the summer haze at Keld farm, and still wearing its Alpha Line Wessex Trains livery, 158 872 leads a Carlisle to Leeds service. In the background the outline of Cross Fell and the North Pennines can just be made out.

Above and below: Two winter pictures taken at Appleby station. The picture above shows 158 908 arriving from Leeds on 2 December 2008, and below 158 853 arriving from Carlisle on 7 February 2009. The tracks going off to the right behind the train were the connection to the now closed line to Penrith and Darlington but is now just sidings.

158 792 is seen soon after leaving Appleby crossing the bridge over the slip road from the A66 at Causey Brow on 20 September 2008 with a train for Leeds.

A Leeds to Carlisle service, with 158 849 bringing up the rear, approaches the 2,629-yard-long Blea Moor Tunnel on 5 August 2009. Note the spoil heaps above the tunnel left behind from when the tunnel was bored.

This page and opposite page: Four pictures taken at Glasgow Queen Street station on 20 February 2009. The picture at the top of this page shows a general view of the seven-platform station with Class 156, 170 and 158 units waiting to depart. Bottom, 170 402 with a recently arrived service from Edinburgh is alongside 158 718 just arrived from Anniesland. Opposite page above, 170 472 has disgorged its passengers and will soon depart back to Cumbernauld. Opposite below 170 423 is about to tackle the 1 in 41 gradient through the Cowlairs Tunnel on its way to Edinburgh.

TransPennine 185 120, working a Cleethorpes to Manchester Airport service, passes the closed Brockelsby station on 16 September 2009. The station closed in October 1993 and, along with the signal box, has been made a Grade II listed building.

Just up the line at Barnetby on 16 September 2009, East Midlands 153 311 arrives with a Newark North Gate to Grimsby Town service. The semaphore signals on this section of line were replaced by colour lights in January 2016.

Above and below: Two pictures taken at Knaresborough. The picture above, taken on 27 May 2008, shows a York to Leeds train formed of a Class 142 leaving the station and crossing the viaduct over the River Nidd on a wet morning. Below, in better weather, 155 342 departs from the station over the level crossing and passes the unique signal box which was built onto the end of a conveniently placed row of houses in 1873.

Above and below: Two pictures taken at Crosby Garrett on 8 August 2012 of Leeds to Carlisle trains. The picture above shows 158 855 passing the site of the station, which closed on 6 October 1952. Below, photographed from the churchyard of St Andrew's Church, two Class 158 units cross the viaduct with the village of Crosby Garrett in the foreground.

A Carlisle to Leeds train crosses the Long Marton Viaduct, which is unfortunately obscured by trees which have grown over the years. Taken on 14 April 2010.

A Carlisle-bound train, with 153 360 bringing up the rear, passes under the farm bridge at Keld on 2 March 2011.

158 855 passes spring blossom and gorse bushes at Causey Brow shortly after leaving Appleby on its way to Leeds on 21 May 2011.

On a foggy winter's afternoon, passengers make for the exit after a day's shopping in the Sales at Carlisle as 158 860 is about to depart from Appleby for Leeds on 28 January 2012.

142 036 waits to leave platform one at Manchester Piccadilly station with an afternoon departure to Rose Hill on 22 May 2012.

At Manchester Oxford Road station 142 018 is on its way to Manchester Airport on 23 August 2011. There has been a station here since 1849, and the current one was built in 1960 to an unusual design as it is constructed largely from wood, which has resulted in it becoming a Grade II listed building.

A Barrow to Manchester Airport train departs from Manchester Deansgate station on 23 August 2011. It is only a short distance to Oxford Road station, which can be seen in the distance.

Overlooking the Bridgewater Canal and the junction between Castle Street and Deansgate, 156 426 heads an eastbound train towards Piccadilly station on 23 August 2011.

There is snow on northern hills as an afternoon Carlisle to Leeds train, with 158 815 leading, passes Keld farm with a wintry sun shining on the backdrop of the North Pennines on 18 February 2012.

Further south on the same day, another Carlisle to Leeds train with 158 795 leading 153 358 leaves the short 181-yard-long Crosby Garrett Tunnel.

Above and below: Two pictures taken at Appleby station. The picture above shows 158 861 entering the station with a northbound service passing 4979 *Wootton Hall* on 2 June 2012. 4979 was sold by BR to Woodhams at Barry for scrap in 1964, and was purchased by the Furness Railway Trust in 1986. It was at Appleby from 9 March 2007 until October 2014 and is now being restored at the Ribble Valley Railway. Also in the picture is the water crane and tank house, which were installed in 1991 to service the regular steam specials that use the S&C. The picture below shows 158 908 and 158 784 passing the tank house with a train for Leeds on 11 April 2014.

On 26 July 2008 TransPennine 185 120 calls at Arnside with a Barrow to Manchester Airport train. In the background is the Kent Estuary, with the Lakeland hills beyond.

TransPennine 185 127 arrives at Oxenholme, which is the junction for Windermere, with a Manchester to Edinburgh train on 22 May 2012.

Above and below: Two pictures taken at Preston station on 16 April 2014. The picture above shows the north end of the station with 142 036 departing for Blackpool South. Below, at platform three, 156 460 is standing under the impressive train shed about to leave for Hazel Grove. The station dates from 1880 and was rebuilt by the LNWR and L&YR from the original 1838 North Union Railway station.

South West Trains 159 107 is working an Exeter to Waterloo service, and is seen arriving at Salisbury on 24 August 2017.

At Birmingham New Street station on 1 March 2008, 170 634 departs with a Central Trains service beneath the Grade II listed Rotunda cylindrical building. Completed in 1965 as an office block, it has been redeveloped as apartments.

Above and below: Two pictures of Pacers at Sheffield station on 7 July 2015. The picture above shows 142 090 waiting to depart for Adwick, and below 144 004 arrives with a service to Doncaster. Until 1970 there were two stations in Sheffield, the other being Victoria station, which was opened in 1851 but closed in 1970, after which all traffic was transferred to this station, which was opened by the Midland Railway in 1870.

TransPennine received nine Class 170 units in 2006 to operate the Hull to Manchester Airport service on which they operated until transferred to Chiltern Trains in 2016. On 4 December 2014, 170 304 is seen at Doncaster with a Hull to Manchester Airport train, while at platform four, a Class 185 is on a Manchester to Cleethorpes service.

On 15 July 2013 150 134 waits in platform eight at York station to leave for Leeds via Harrogate. This service was worked by Pacers for many years, but recently Class 170s have taken over from the Class 150s.

Two of the next pictures were taken at the remaining intermediate stations on the Hull to Scarborough line to retain an overall roof, so beloved of the North Eastern Railway. At Filey station, which was opened in 1846, 158 795 calls with a Sheffield to Scarborough service on 4 August 2015. The original NER footbridge also still survives and is unusual as it disappears through the retaining wall to reach the exit.

Another station with a NER footbridge is Cottingham, where 158 860 stops with a Hull to Bridlington service on 3 November 2014. The original goods shed still survives in private use, and is visible above the front of the train.

Dating from 1846, Beverley is the other station with an overall roof, and also has a NER covered footbridge. This recent picture shows 170 459 with a Scarborough to Sheffield train on 21 October 2021.

Looking in the other direction at Beverley, 158 861 departs for Hull on 6 August 2015 past the NER signal box and over the level crossing.

165 127 stands in Didcot station with an Oxford to Paddington train on 24 August 2017. The recently installed overhead electric wires have yet to reach Oxford, hence the diesel-powered train. In the background the replica GWR Steam Railcar can be glimpsed in the Railway Centre.

Further west at Cardiff station there is no sign of the impending electrification as 175 114 waits for departure with an Arriva Trains Wales service for Holyhead on 23 July 2018.

Above and below: Above, on the same day, 150 432 arrives in Cardiff station with a train for Bargoed, and below 158 961 waits to leave in the direction of Swansea and 143 606 is bound for Merthyr Tydfil.

Above and below: The next four pictures were taken at Newport on 23 July 2018, where the first supports for the overhead wires have appeared, with electric services due to begin in 2020. Two GWR Cardiff to Portsmouth Harbour trains are seen, with the picture above showing 150 248-207 departing, and below the guard waits for the all clear to start 158 961 on its way.

Above and below: At platform two Arriva Trains Wales 158 841 will soon be leaving for Fishguard Harbour, to be followed by 170 117 with a CrossCountry service from Nottingham to Cardiff. Both taken on 23 July 2018. The remains of the footbridge have now been demolished.

Above and below: Two pictures taken at Levenshulme on 31 May 2019. The picture above shows 175 103 passing with a Manchester to Milford Haven service, and below 156 470 and 158 857 head for Liverpool with a service from Norwich.

142 049, working a Manchester Piccadilly to Alderley Edge train, calls at Heaton Chapel station on 31 May 2019.

One of the new CAF-built DMUs, 195 116, waits in platform ten at Crewe station for its next duty on 8 June 2019. Fifty-eight two- and three-car sets have been delivered to Northern, and were built in Spain and Newport, South Wales.

Above and below: Two pictures taken at Crewe station on 10 June 2019. The picture above shows Transport for Wales 150 242 standing in platform eight, and below 175 114 waits to depart with a Manchester to Carmarthen service. Although dating back to 1837, the station still manages to retain many of its original features despite its many owners over nearly two centuries.

Above and below: Two pictures taken at Shrewsbury station. Above, West Midlands Railway 170 630 waits to depart with a service for Birmingham New Street on 4 June 2019. Below, Transport for Wales 158 825 is the lead unit on this Cambrian Coast service for Aberystwyth and Pwllheli, waiting to leave on 8 June 2019. Shrewsbury station is another with a long history dating back to 1846. It was built for the Shrewsbury & Chester Railway, and the main building has been given Grade II listed status.

158 821 calls at Minffordd station on its way to Pwllheli on 6 June 2019. This station also offers connections to the narrow-gauge Ffestiniog Railway, with some of its rolling stock visible in the background.

At the terminus of the Cambrian Coast line at Pwllheli on 4 June 2019, 158 333 waits to depart with the 17.42 to Machynlleth. The station here was opened by the Cambrian Railway in 1909, replacing the original 1867 station.

Above and below: Two pictures taken at Smethwick Galton Bridge station on 9 June 2019. The picture above shows 172 212 departing for Worcester Foregate Street, and below 172 212 leaves with a train for Stratford-upon-Avon. The station was opened in 1995 as part of the scheme to reopen the Jewellery line across Birmingham, and is on two levels, with the Birmingham to Wolverhampton line at the lower level.

To celebrate the 2014 Tour de France cycle race, which started in Leeds and spent two days in Yorkshire, Northern Trains ran 158 849 in yellow Le Tour colours celebrating the event, and it is seen here arriving at Gare de Hutton Cranswick on 8 January 2015 with a Bridlington to Hull train.

On 16 January 2019, 950001, the Network Rail Track Recording Train, ran from Scarborough to Hull and back, and is seen here passing through Hutton Cranswick station on its way to Hull.

Scotrail 158 871 calls at Hutton Cranswick with a Bridlington to Hull service on 2 October 2018. With the opening of the Edinburgh to Glasgow electrification, many Scotrail Class 158 and 170 DMUs were redundant, and some found their way south to Northern, and in a major reorganisation of units which included the withdrawal of the Pacers, some finished up on the East Yorkshire Coast line.

A late afternoon Bridlington to Hull service formed of 158 903 heads south across the flat East Yorkshire countryside soon after departing from Hutton Cranswick on 21 October 2015.

Above and below: The Pacer trains nodded their way into the history books in 2020 after some thirty-five years of service, and these four pictures are my last of the type. Both pictures on this page were taken at Doncaster, and the picture above is of 144 005 departing for Lincoln on 26 October 2016, and below 142 066 leaves for Sheffield on 27 February 2019. 144 005 is now with Loram Rail, and 142 066 was scrapped at Newport Docks.

Beauty and the beast at York on 19 January 2019. On the left Azuma 800 103 has just arrived from Kings Cross, and on the right 142 086 won't get to Newcastle from that platform without a reversal. 142 086 was broken up at Wye Valley Metals of Hereford in August 2020.

My very last Pacer picture was this shot of 144 008 waiting to depart from Doncaster for Sheffield on 8 February 2020. The nearest coach 55831 has gone to Corby Model Railway Society, and the front one 55808 to Fagley Primary School in Bradford.

Another of the recently arrived Scotrail units, 170 455, stands in York station with a service to Leeds via Harrogate on 21 September 2019.

185 138 passes the Singleton Birch Lime Works as it approaches Barnetby with a Cleethorpes to Manchester service on 30 October 2019.

Looking in the other direction, 170 511 climbs away from Barnetby with a Leicester to Grimsby train on 15 June 2022.

East Midland Railway 156 917 arrives at Barnetby station with an afternoon Grimsby Town to Leicester service on 15 June 2022. The famous semaphore signals have recently been replaced by modern LED colour lights, but the former Great Central Railway East signal box still survives, although out of use.

On the Settle to Carlisle line, 158 752 approaches Kirkby Stephen with a Leeds to Carlisle service on 7 October 2022.

At Arram station 155 344 arrives with a Bridlington to York train on 15 October 2021.

At the other end of Arram station another Bridlington to York train departs on 25 November 2021 formed of 155 346. Arram station has the platforms staggered either side of a central level crossing.

In a later reorganisation, the seven remaining Class 155 units were concentrated at Hull for use on the Bridlington to York service, and 155 341 is seen here departing from Brough with one of these trains on 21 October 2021.

Class 170 454, still wearing its Scotrail livery, waits to depart from Bridlington with the 19.27 service to Hull on 18 June 2019.

170 458 runs into Bridlington with a Sheffield to Scarborough service on 22 October 2021. The train is running past major work being carried out to convert the signalling to colour lights, and to renew the junction trackwork, which was completed on 31 October 2021. The new panel to control the revised layout was installed in the old NER signal box, which can be seen to the rear of the train.

Another type of unit that was drafted in when the Pacers were withdrawn was the Class 150, and two units, 150 276 and 150 135, stand in Hull station on 21 April 2019. The picture shows the two differing types of 150 – with and without corridor connections.

At York station 195 109 departs from platform ten for Leeds on 14 June 2022. In platform nine a TPE Class 802 is heading north with a Liverpool to Newcastle train.